Little People, BIG DREAMS™
LEWIS HAMILTON

Written by
Maria Isabel Sánchez Vegara

Illustrated by
Fernando Martín

Frances Lincoln
Children's Books

Once, in the south of England, lived a boy called Lewis. His parents split up when he was two, and he lived with his mother and two sisters, but he spent many weekends with his dad—watching Formula One racing on television.

For Lewis's fifth birthday, his father gave him a remote-controlled car. Being the only Black child and the youngest racer wasn't easy because some drivers picked on him. Yet, Lewis always followed his dad's advice: let your results speak for you.

Soon, Lewis was beating any grown-up on the track. When he earned his first two trophies, he and his dad celebrated by eating noodle soup and bacon sandwiches on the back of their car. Never before had he felt so proud of himself!

The following Christmas, Lewis got the most amazing present:
a go-kart! It was pretty old, but his father fixed it for
him and made him a promise: as long as Lewis worked
hard at school, he would support his son's racing.

His dad took on extra jobs to keep his promise, and Lewis never missed a day at school either. Still, racing was so expensive that sometimes he couldn't make it to the next competition.

All of the family's money went into buying tires and fuel, and they didn't have a penny to spend on anything special. But all that sacrifice paid off when Lewis was ten. He became the youngest driver to win the British Kart Championship!

That year, he was invited to a big racing event. There, he introduced himself to Ron Dennis, who was the boss of McLaren, Lewis's favorite car racing team.

Lewis asked him for a place on his team and an autograph that he kept forever.

Luckily, Lewis didn't have to wait that long. Three years later, he earned his place as the youngest driver ever to join McLaren's Young Driver Support Programme. Soon, he was showing his amazing talent in fast racing competitions.

For his debut as a Formula One driver, Lewis wore a bright yellow helmet to honor his hero, Ayrton Senna.

When he turned on the engine and the wheels began to spin,
everyone at the team knew a future champion was on the track.

During his rookie season, Lewis ended up second in the World Driver's Championship. And the following year, he didn't just become the first Black driver to top the Formula One rankings, but its youngest champion ever.

Winning race after race and title after title, Lewis broke the record for most Formula One triumphs and, after his seventh World Driver's Championship, he was knighted. Yet Sir Lewis has never forgotten who he is and where he came from.

Lewis travels the world to encourage children to dream of a better future.

He works to break down barriers in motorsports
so that other Black children will one day
become engineers, car mechanics, or drivers.

And every time he puts his helmet on, little Lewis shows that it is a sport that should be open to everyone.

Because we've all got what it takes to win. We just need to show the world what we can do.

LEWIS HAMILTON

(Born 1985)

1995

2008

Sir Lewis Carl Hamilton was born in Stevenage, England, in 1985. His
parents separated when he was two and he split his time between them.
Growing up, he experienced racist bullying at school, which left him feeling
hurt and frustrated. His dad gave him a go-kart when Lewis was seven,
and told him: "Let your results speak louder than anything you have to say."
Lewis's driving career began when he was eight and, two years later, he
won the British Kart Championship. Soon after, he joined the McLaren
Young Driver Support Programme. At 15, he became the youngest ever
driver to be ranked number one at go-karting. Lewis quickly progressed
to car racing and, in a championship in 2003, he won 10 of the 15
races he entered! He was signed up to the McLaren Formula One team

2019

2022

signed up to the McLaren Formula One team in 2007, becoming the first and, so far, only Black driver to race in the Grand-Prix series. The following year, at the age of 23, he won the world title, becoming the youngest ever winner. Lewis has since triumphed at many Grand-Prix races and, alongside Michael Schumacher, holds the joint record for winning the most World Drivers' Championships. Using his fame, Lewis speaks publicly about racism, LGBTQ+ rights, children's welfare, and animal and environmental concerns, and he pushes for increased diversity in motorsports. In 2020, he received a knighthood from the UK's Prince of Wales for his outstanding achievements. A global icon, Lewis teaches us that we all have what it takes to win, regardless of what others may think.

Want to find out more about **Lewis Hamilton?**

Have a read of this great book:

Lewis Hamilton Rules by Simon Mugford and Dan Green

Brimming with creative inspiration, how-to projects, and useful information to enrich your everyday life, quarto.com is a favorite destination for those pursuing their interests and passions.

Text © 2023 Maria Isabel Sánchez Vegara. Illustrations © 2023 Fernando Martín.

"Little People, BIG DREAMS" and "Pequeña & Grande" are trademarks of Alba Editorial S.L.U. and/or Beautifool Couple S.L.

First Published in the UK in 2023 by Frances Lincoln Children's Books, an imprint of The Quarto Group.

100 Cummings Center, Suite 265D, Beverly, MA 01915, USA

T +1 978-282-95900 **www.Quarto.com**

Any faults are the publisher's, who will be happy to rectify for future printings.

A catalogue record for this book is available from the Library of Congress.

ISBN 978-0-7112-8316-9

Set in Futura BT.

Published by Peter Marley • Designed by Lyli Feng and Sasha Moxon

Commissioned by Lucy Menzies • Edited by Lucy Menzies and Rachel Robinson • Production by Nikki Ingram

Manufactured in Guangdong, China CC102022

1 3 5 7 9 8 6 4 2

Photographic acknowledgements (pages 28-29, from left to right): 1. British Junior Go Kart racer, Lewis Hamilton, aged 10, ready for a drive at Kimbolton race track in England, 19th December 1995. © Philip Brown/Popperfoto via Getty Images. 2. NORTHAMPTON, UNITED KINGDOM - JULY 06: Lewis Hamilton of Great Britain and McLaren Mercedes celebrates on the podium after winning the British Formula One Grand Prix at Silverstone on July 6, 2008 in Northampton, England. © Paul Gilham via Getty Images. 3. F1 World Champion, Mercedes' British driver Lewis Hamilton, delivers a press conference in Sao Paulo, Brazil, on November 13, 2019, ahead of the upcoming Formula One Brazilian Grand Prix on November 17. © NELSON ALMEDIA/PA via Getty Images. 4. BUDAPEST, HUNGARY - JULY 31: lh during the F1 Grand Prix of Hungary at Hungaroring on July 31, 2022 in Budapest, Hungary. © Peter J Fox via Getty Images.

MIX
Paper | Supporting responsible forestry
FSC® C008047

Collect the *Little People,* **BIG DREAMS™** series:

FRIDA KAHLO 	COCO CHANEL 	MAYA ANGELOU	AMELIA EARHART	AGATHA CHRISTIE	MARIE CURIE	ROSA PARKS	AUDREY HEPBURN
EMMELINE PANKHURST 	ELLA FITZGERALD 	ADA LOVELACE	JANE AUSTEN	GEORGIA O'KEEFFE	HARRIET TUBMAN	ANNE FRANK 	MOTHER TERESA
JOSEPHINE BAKER	L. M. MONTGOMERY	JANE GOODALL 	SIMONE DE BEAUVOIR	MUHAMMAD ALI	STEPHEN HAWKING 	MARIA MONTESSORI	VIVIENNE WESTWOOD 
MAHATMA GANDHI	DAVID BOWIE	WILMA RUDOLPH	DOLLY PARTON	BRUCE LEE 	RUDOLF NUREYEV	ZAHA HADID	MARY SHELLEY
MARTIN LUTHER KING JR.	DAVID ATTENBOROUGH 	ASTRID LINDGREN 	EVONNE GOOLAGONG	BOB DYLAN 	ALAN TURING	BILLIE JEAN KING	GRETA THUNBERG
JESSE OWENS	JEAN-MICHEL BASQUIAT 	ARETHA FRANKLIN	CORAZON AQUINO 	PELÉ	ERNEST SHACKLETON	STEVE JOBS	AYRTON SENNA
LOUISE BOURGEOIS	ELTON JOHN	JOHN LENNON	PRINCE	CHARLES DARWIN	CAPTAIN TOM MOORE	HANS CHRISTIAN ANDERSEN	STEVIE WONDER

MEGAN RAPINOE

MARY ANNING

MALALA YOUSAFZAI

ANDY WARHOL

RUPAUL

MICHELLE OBAMA

MINDY KALING

IRIS APFEL

ROSALIND FRANKLIN

RUTH BADER GINSBURG

MARILYN MONROE

KAMALA HARRIS

ALBERT EINSTEIN

CHARLES DICKENS

YOKO ONO

MICHAEL JORDAN

NELSON MANDELA

PABLO PICASSO

AMANDA GORMAN

GLORIA STEINEM

FLORENCE NIGHTINGALE

HARRY HOUDINI

J.R.R. TOLKIEN

ELVIS PRESLEY

NEIL ARMSTRONG

ALEXANDER VON HUMBOLDT

NIKOLA TESLA

WILMA MANKILLER

MARCUS RASHFORD

LAVERNE COX

MAE JEMISON

DWAYNE JOHNSON

HELEN KELLER

ANNA PAVLOVA

QUEEN ELIZABETH

TERRY FOX

HEDY LAMARR

SHAKIRA

FREDDIE MERCURY

LEWIS HAMILTON

LOUIS PASTEUR

PRINCESS DIANA

ACTIVITY BOOKS

STICKER ACTIVITY BOOK

COLORING BOOK

LITTLE ME, BIG DREAMS JOURNAL

Discover more about the series at www.littlepeoplebigdreams.com